DOUBLE TAKE

BY JEROME BEATTY, JR.

CARTOONS BY TERENCE PARKES (LARRY)
(LARRY) CARTOONS BY TERENCE PARKES
PARKES (LARRY) CARTOONS BY TERENCE
TERENCE PARKES (LARRY) CARTOONS BY
BY TERENCE PARKES (LARRY) CARTOONS

THE STEPHEN GREENE PRESS, BRATTLEBORO, VERMONT *
VERMONT * THE STEPHEN GREENE PRESS, BRATTLEBORO,
BRATTLEBORO, VERMONT * THE STEPHEN GREENE PRESS,
PRESS, BRATTLEBORO, VERMONT * THE STEPHEN GREENE
GREENE PRESS, BRATTLEBORO, VERMONT * THE STEPHEN

aoin shrdlu etaoin shrdlu etaoin shrdlu etaoin shrdlu etaoin shrdlu etaoin shrdlu eta

This book has been produced in the United States of America:
designed by Janet Greene, printed and bound by The Book Press.

It is published by The Stephen Greene Press, Brattleboro,
Vermont 05301

Library of Congress Catalog Card Number: 71-173399
International Standard Book Number: 0-8289-0143-0

INTORDUCTION

People are constantly trying to pass along news, instructions, information and warnings to other people. So many words appear in print every day that there are bound to be some funny results—and the mistakes are passed along, too. It's interesting to read in the Bloomington, Indiana, paper that "Paul Ford once worked as a proof-reader in Philadtlphia." Or a warning in a Long Island supermarket ad: "Not responsible for typeogarphical errors." The experts are no better than anyone else. I received a "Calandar of Events" from Eastern Oregon College, and an announcement from Massachusetts of an Academic Awards Banquet in the "High Scool Gym."

It's when Americans are printing signs that they are happiest, especially with a *Keep Out,* to which they feel they have to add POSITIVELY, and then, just to make sure, THIS MEANS YOU. They also love to post a *No Tresspasing,* or a *No Admitance,* improving them occasionally by making an *N* backwards.

But you don't have to be a good speller to appreciate the goofs collected here. A highway sign for a service station/restaurant reads "Eat Here and Get Gas," which was probably done on purpose, who can tell? A headline like POPE'S MOTORCADE

STONED takes on a special meaning these days. When you read that two bandits in Norwalk, Connecticut, "made their getaway in a parked auto," you realize why crime pays. Think of the gas they saved.

I have gathered all the silly things I've seen in newspapers, on signs, and elsewhere, added those that friends have given me, and put them together here as a contribution to English literature. If you get a few laughs out of *Double Cake,* it will have been well worth the effrot. Keep your eyes pealed for this sort of thing. It makes life worth loving. J.B.

NUTTY
NOTICES

Sammy Davis, Jr.

Richard Burton &

Elizabeth Taylor

In their first public appearance together since their marriage

—Theater marquee in St. Louis

STAND FIRM AMERICA bumper stickers for sale
Satisfaction guaranteed or money refunded within ten days.

— New York City

To keep from getting complaints about the free
service, there will be no more free service

— New York gas station

All vegetables served in this hotel were
washed in water passed by the head chef

— Akasaka, Japan

These books were owned by a little old
lady who never read faster than fifty
words a minute

— Louisville second-hand bookstore

At the Golden Pagoda, Rangoon:

TO TOUCH MEANS INSTANT DEATH.
ANYONE CAUGHT WILL BE PRO-
SECUTED TO THE FULL EXTENT OF
THE LAW

– Indiana power station

In case of emergency (1) do not be alarmed
(2) push the alarm button

– Pueblo, Colo., elevator

In the window of an appliance shop in Alton, Ill.:

STOP THIS INHUMAN EMBALMING–
RENT AN ELECTRIC REFRIGERATED CASKET

Henry James Hairdressing Establishment

– Wardour Street, London

If you don't go away and leave me alone,
I'll find someone who will

– LaGrande, Ore., shop

Store near Mt. Fujiyama: You'll be freezed by our coldest beer in town.

On a Tokyo billboard: Go one mile, more down, Number One Car Wash.

At a Yokohama shop: What you can't get on the high seas sure is plentiful here.

In little old New England, north of Concord, N.H. is the –

COUNTRY STORE DISCOUNT HOUSE

Posted by an arithmetically weak store proprietor
in White Plains, N.Y.:

Buy Now: Lowest Discounts on All Appliances and T.V.

NOTICE

NO THOROUGHFARE

PRIVATE PROPERTY

All persons warned against trespassing.

New, abnormal, and undisclosed

Sources of DANGER constantly arising.

—Placed by the Susquehanna Electric Company on
the south shore of the Susquehanna River
several miles upstream from Havre de Grace,
Md. (Are they trying to tell us something?)

— Brownsville, Pa.

During the brewery strike in New York, the Daily
News headlined the story about the breakdown of
negotiations:

STILL AT LAGERHEADS

More Daily News headlines:

Switzerland rejects Moscow protest over expulsion of two spies:

RUSSIAN COMPLAINT FULL OF HOLES, SAY SWISS

In New York a truckload of dresses is hijacked:

$50,000 WORTH OF LADIES SKIRTS LIFTED

Mickey Rooney, who had been married four times, wed again:

HALF-PINT TAKES A FIFTH

Store window in Washington, D.C. during August:

REMOVAL SALE
LADIES PANTIES
4 for $1

—*New York City*

Alterations

Men and Ladies

— Great Falls, Mont.

GAME SUNDAY

John XXIII

vs.

Our Lady

PORK SHOP SPECIAL--
OCEAN FRESH TO YOU

Simsbury, Conn., store

— Cambridge, Mass.

Just inside of the Woolworth's in Harrisburg, Pa., is a stack of self-service baskets with the sign: For Your Use and Convenience While in Our Store. *One day the baskets were piled full of toilet tissue.*

On a saloon being renovated in Grand Rapids:

KEEP OUT! SEE?

No Dumping Selectmen

—Amesbury, Mass.

Get Yours in the Narthex

*— Watertown, N.Y., church bulletin board,
asking parishioners to pick up envelopes*

Remington Township Dump
Residence Only

— Remington, Wis.

Hatching Frocks

— Massachusetts maternity shop

Near a school in Geary County, Kan.:

Please drive carefully—Don't run over
the children—Wait for the teacher

*Electric sign that once stood high over the Fort
Worth station of the Texas & Pacific Railroad,
which was proud of the special brand of coffee
served in its restaurant and dining cars:*

DRINK T&P COFFEE

Welcome GOP Delegates
Wrestling
Lippizan Stallions

— Milwaukee Arena marquee

In a Dublin bookstore:

There are over 8,000 books banned in
Eire. If by chance we have one on display,
please inform us and it will be destroyed.

In Niantic, Conn:

Green crabs for
Black fishing,
Whiting for
Bluefishing.

DRIVE CAREFUL — BRIDGE OUT

— Bloomfield, Conn.

"Aqui Se Habla Yiddish"

– Reported as in store windows in Miami and New York

– At water hazard of golf course on Hilton Head Island, S.C.

NOT AN ACCREDITED EGRESS DOOR

–Ritz Carlton (Boston) lobby
revolving door

CAUTION: WILD CHILDREN

– Greenfield, N.H.

Drive Carefully – We'll Wait

– New Mexico tombstone dealer .

A Washington, D.C., newsstand/bookstore discourages browsers.

WE CANNOT TOLERATE EXCESSIVE READING

> To move the cabin, push the button of the wishing floor. If the cabin enter more persons, each should press the button of the wishing floor. Driving is then going by natural order.
>
> — *Elevator in Hotel Slavija, Belgrade.*

Dry Cleaner, Schenectady, N.Y.:

ONE HOUR SUDDEN SERVICE

> NO LEFT TURN 4 to 6 P.M.
> Except busses Except Sat. & Sun.
>
> — *Garfield, N.J., intersection*

> OLNEY INN
> OPEN ALL YEAR
> Except February
> (Closed Mondays)
>
> —*Olney, Md.*

At Atlanta's Hilton Inn:

> SWIMMING POOL IS FOR MOTEL
> GUESTS ONLY PLEASE REGISTER
> WITH THE LIFE GUARD (No life guard
> on duty. Swim at Your Own Risk)

More Nipponese troubles with English:

In a Tokyo hotel: There is a nice lobby on the
second floor. Please have more relax up there.

On a trash can:

At the night table bell: Right Away Boy.

By a hook on the wall: Place key here after using
door.

On the menu:

> Glill Room
>
> Shriced Bananas

The card catalog in a Washington (state) library had this entry: SEX: (see librarian). *After complaints about the taste of the wording, the card was changed to read:* SEX: (For sex ask at desk).

CARNICERIA EL MORO

Formerly

KATZ KOSHER MARKET

—Store in Miami

For Rent, Sleeping Room For Man

For Sale, Maternity Dresses

— Fort Smith, Ark.

MEN ROOMS ONLY. NO WOMEN ALOUD.

NOR NO WHISKEY SOLD HERE.

— Birmingham, Ala., rooming house

Headline of New York Times article telling how the previously untilled areas in Soviet Kazakhstan have for the fourth year failed to fulfill the grain delivery plan:

SOVIET VIRGIN LANDS
SHORT OF GOAL AGAIN

In the Hayden Planetarium, near stairs on the second floor:

To Solar System and Rest Rooms —

– In Vancouver, B.C.

In a music store, an album of a rock star had a strip of cellophane across the picture of the singer that read: Sealed for your protection.

Poster in a cheap London bookshop that specializes in sexy books, and somehow acquired a stock of Little Women:

"Four Young Girls Tell All"

At a laundry next door to Tacoma, Wash., theater where I Am Curious (Yellow) was showing:

You may hide in here until showtime

Criminal Registration Required

— *Atlantic City boundary*

On the menu of a Mandarin restaurant in New York:

"NO—NO—NO Chop Suey!"

Deposit Used Blades Here
See America First

— Los Angeles hotel bathroom

SUGGESTIVE MOTHER'S DAY GIFTS

— Dare, Va., department store

In a Brooklyn barber shop:

"I need your head to run my business"

Please take lost children to the
Lion House

— Washington, D.C., zoo

Easy To Lay Yourself

— Edinburgh carpet store

Atlantic City barbershop:

"Haircutting with ambidexter velocity"

"The famous writer Chateaubriand was leaving here from 1810 to 1816.."

— Hotel du Pas de Calais, Paris

Church for sale
Buy now, Pray later.

— Arvada, Colo.

"Self Service Advisory Center"

— 242 Tottenham Court Road, London

Dainty Rubbish Service

— Avon, Conn.

NO TREE CLIMBING OR THROWING

— *Washington, Tex., state park*

Worms Parking in Rear

— *Illinois tackle shop*

I May Be Slow
But I'm Ahead of You

—*On rear of old truck*

Mo trespasing without pernission

— *Pennsylvania empty lot*

FEED CHILDREN HERE

— Hole in link fence around the Ebro, Fla., dog track.
(Parents pass food through to minors not allowed inside.)

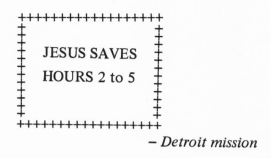

```
+++++++++++++++++++
+                 +
+   JESUS SAVES   +
+                 +
+   HOURS 2 to 5  +
+                 +
+                 +
+                 +
+++++++++++++++++++
```

– Detroit mission

"This is to advise you that we have this day CHARGED YOUR ACCOUNT as follows: $4,430.66. Please turn over for breakdown."

– Notice sent by Long Island bank

Vienna Airport coin-operated lockers:

1. Please read the printed instructions on baggage box.
2. Throw down the coins slowly. Take care that the first coin has fallen down before throwing in the second coin.
3. Baggage which is larger than the baggage box cannot be put in because of disturbance.
4. Informations will be given at the information desk.

FINE FOR DUMPING

> — *West Virginia cemetery*

COOL IT   Ice Cold Ice
Blind
Driveway   — *Cape Cod*

> *—Mashpee, Mass.*

DRINKING, DANCING OR PETTING

> — *Yokosuka, Japan, bar*

Courteous, Efficient Self-Service

> — *Ann Arbor cafeteria*

W.O. HART MEMORIAL PARK
In Memory of W.O. Hart

> — *Orange, Cal.*

Any unauthorized cars will be spirited away

— Johannesburg church parking lot

THIS IS THE WRONG ROAD TO CHATTANOOGA

*— Atlanta gas station one block north of where
the northbound highway takes a sharp turn*

No smoking except in lounge end only

— Penn Central coach

HAVE YOUR NEXT AFFAIR HERE

— Holiday Inn marquee

Colorado Springs Travel Bureau:

"Please Go Away"

Employees must wash hands
before leaving the management.

– Greenwich Village bar

Tubby's Sugar Shack
Topless Dancers
(Coats and Ties Requested)

– Richmond, Va.

– Washington Island, Lake Michigan

Emergency Exit —— Not To Be Used
Under Any Circumstances

– Sterling, Colo., factory

READING POPULAR,
SAY LIBRARIANS

– Greensboro (N.C.) News

— Ascutney, Vt., greenhouse

Private Property. Welcome

— New Mexico

We Have Button-Fly Levis
Open 'Til 10 P.M. Tonight

— Boston store

Only Low Talk Permitted Here

— Boston Public Library

You haven't lived unless you have bought a house
in Orange Gardens! This is a community for young
adults. People on their way up. Sorry, no pets or
children.

— California development

Personal Loan Applications in Mezzanine.

No Waiting For Seats.

— New York bank

— New Hope, Pa., farm.

Clam Chowder $.50

Texas-size Bowl $.25

— Alaska restaurant

No Trip To Small

No Trip To Large

— Wichita, Kan., travel agency

Nikko Botanical Gardens

Admission by Ticket Only

No Botanizing, Drinking and Uproaring, etc.

In the Garden

— Tokyo

It Is A Federal Offense
To Assault A Postal Employee
(While on Duty)

– U.S. post offices

I'd give my right arm to be ambidextrous.

– *Big Sur graffito*

Due to operational difficulties, Chicago will not burn today.

– *Amusement park*

For Sale: Handmade, embroidered
clothes for animals of all kinds.
Specialize in outfits for monkeys.

– *College Park, Md.*

Authenticity At Its Best!

– *Ouray, Colo., Western Museum*

SHOPLIFTERS STAY OUT
WE KNOW YOU BY SIGHT

– Madison Avenue curio shop

We don't mangle your clothes by machinery. We do it by hand.

– New York laundry

When boys and girls cooperate, production goes much faster.

– Shanghai factory

Headline on story of marriage of Paul Winchell:

Ventriloquist Caught Moving Lips

HONGKONG RESTAURANT
CHINESE-SPANISH-AMERICAN FOOD

– Miami

T-bone $.49

With Meat $2.98

— St. Louis restaurant

Self-drive Undertaker

— Killarney, Ireland

Out to Lunch

If Not Back by 5–

Out To Dinner Also

—Reading, Mass.

— Moline, Ill., flower shop's Mother's Day special

Your marriage Should Be Within Twelve Months

of Your booking.

—London's Hotel Eden (offering discount to honeymooners)

Crisp combination salad tossed in your room

– Rabat Hilton menu

CHICKEN LITTLE WAS RIGHT

– California air-raid shelter

ON SALE
White Muslim Bedsheets

– New York store

WE FIX ALL KINDS OF REPAIRS

– N.Y.C. electric appliance store

USED FOOD PURVEYORS

– Ft. Lauderdale garbage truck

Members are cautioned not to play cards with members

–New York Club

Reserved for   Reserved for   Reserved for
Commanding   Visiting   Any
General   General   2d Lieutenant

—Fort Sam Houston parking lot

—Town in Kansas

Eyes Examined While You Wait

— Auburn, Pa., optometrist

From a fortune cookie in a Chinese restaurant in
N.Y.C.:

"Disregard previous cookie"

Exclusively devoted to the manufacturers
of dual purpose sleeping equipment.

— Bedding (trade paper) motto

Immaculate Conception Maternity Hospital

— Manila

Theater of the Four Seasons
(Closed for the Winter)

— Long Island, N.Y.

We beg your attention, please

PASSANGER GENTLEMAN: You may
be a carrier of the grippal disease. In protection of your health and in order to
avoid its propagation, we beg you that
in the case to show yourself in the next
seventy two (72) hours temperature or
general malaise, SEND FOR THE DOC-
TOR AND REMAIN AT HOME. More-
over we pray you to communicate that
novelty by phones: 30-0220 y 33- 3311
(Department of Sanitary Emergency).

*— La Paz airport, during
Asian 'flu scare*

— Long Island, N.Y.

SUNDAY IS THE
LORD'S DAY
AND THE
FULNES$ THEIR OF

— Delray, Fla., supermarket

You are Cordially Invited
To a Testimonial Dinner
Honoring The
Honorable Kenneth Cory
Member of the Assembly
California State Legislature
at the Aneheim Convention Center
Garden Grove Room
Donation One Hundred Dollars per person
Roquefort Dressing $.25 Extra

— Formal invitation

Today's Special: Chip & Dale Mirror

— Junction City, Kan.

— Rutherford, N.J., grade crossing

TO ALL EMPLOYEES

Due to increased competition and a keen desire to remain in business, we find it necessary to institute a new policy.

EFFECTIVE IMMEDIATELY

We are asking that somewhere between starting and quitting time and without infringing too much on the time usually devoted to lunch period, story telling, ticket selling, vacation planning, and the rehash of yesterday's TV programs, that each employee find some time that can be set aside and known as the "work break."

To some this may seem a radical innovation, but we honestly believe the idea has great possibilities. It can conceivably be an aid to steady employment and it might also be a means of securing regular pay checks.

While the adoption of the "work break" plan is not compulsory, it is hoped that each employee will find enough time to give it a fair trial.

— East Lansing, Mich.

Motorsport, Inc. assumes no responsibility for cars left for repairs with respect to fire, theft, or acts of God or His representatives.

– Boulder, Colo.

When a girl wears attire which is disruptive to the normal routine of school, this is the type of attire we want to look at a second time.

*–Wisconsin school pronouncement
regarding mini-skirts and hotpants*

Our Lady of Perpetual Help Pawnshop

– Manila

Sanitary Refuse Company: satisfaction guaranteed or double your garbage back

– Wellfleet, Mass.

Delayed inception of office hours of approximately one-half hour is anticipated.

– U. of Nevada

```
ANTIQUES – OLD AND NEW
```

– Arkansas shop

Packed in Japan with diligence and
responsibility. Serve cold or not with
lemon, perhaps. It is assuredly advised
that all who delight with their cocktails
will happily engage in serving this most
sincere brand

– Safari-San Smoked Oyster can

Please do not smoke in bed. Aside from
being a state law, it endangers your life.

– Independence, Kan., motel

Coffins and All Other Requisites

– Killarney, Ireland, shop

No
Police
Parking
Only

— Falmouth, Mass.

No Salesmen Allowed
(Only the Ones I Owe)

— Cleveland

— Connecticut highway

DAILY SPECIAL
Hare Pie $1.75
For the Kiddies: Bunny on a Bun $.75

— Springdale, Nev., inn

TRESPASSERS WILL BE PERSECUTED

— Murray Bay, P.Q.

Regulation 1: Ladies are forbidden to visit the rooms occupied by single men and vice versa. To avoid any inconvenience to the guest, it is requested that visitors convene in the Main Lobby for this purpose.

— El Rio Motel, Nuevo Laredo, Mexico

Reserved: St. John's Sister's

—Parking lot at St. Joseph's Hospital, St. Paul

Now Showing—"Hamlet" by the author of "Romeo and Juliet"

—San Francisco Movie marquee

Only those firms that measure up to rigid standards are invited to become members of the National Selected Morticians.

— San Antonio, Tex.

TRACK THIS FRI
OUR FEILD 3:00

— San Diego high school

FLEA MARKET
(Beware of Dog)

— Georgia

This is the place to void where prohibited

— Kansas City restroom

Smarnmit Restaurant

Have the map with Thai and English for your-tourist of Cholburi. We have cars at your service all the time. It you reach to Smarnmit-restaurant already. If you wish to meet someone or want to-go somewhere or to buy somethings. We pleasure to advice to you always. If your car have object, we have the mender for you. If you want the food already make to your resident. We pleasure to bring to your resident or you want the food go with you for travel we have the box prepare for you all the time.

— Menu in Thailand

Coming events listed on marquee of Detroit's Cobo Hall:

National Funeral Directors Association
American Society of Body Engineers
and
Bye Bye Birdie!

Any Bag in Window
$5.00
More Inside

— Brooklyn, N.Y.

— An inn in rural England

Books are for sale. Please do not read.

— Long Beach, Cal., bus terminal bookstore

The most effective No Trespassing message ever invented is in Gig Harbor, Wash., where a man has posted his property thusly (there are no paths, by the way):

Snake Farm

Keep on The Path

— Grayslake, Ill   animal hospital

OUR BLOOMERS ARE SHOWING

— New Hampshire flower mart

Animals are requested to be quiet whilst
guests are drinking and vice versa

— Tsavo National Park, Kenya

Southern Fried Chicanery

— Chevy Chase, Md., diner

PEDESTRIANS WALKING

> *— Woods Hole, Mass.*

Polynesian
Imitation
Chinese Mustard
Allied Old English, Inc.
Newark, N.J.

> *—Package legend*

Repent Now and Avoid the Rush

> *— Philadelphia church*

Tuesday Night Dance Classes—
Mamboships Now Open

> *— New York dance hall*

"This telephone doesn't work like any
other telephone you have ever used."

— On public phone, Makapuu Beach, Hawaii

"In sickness or in health, your pharmacist is ready to serve you."

Crist Mortuary
"Ask Those We've Served"

— Boulder, Colo.

Contents: 100% miscellaneous by-products of undetermined origin

— Rug label

Men's Socks On Sale!
$.59 A Pair
65% Lamb's Wool and
40% Nylon

— Discount chain store

No Trespassing Unless Permission is Granted

— California campus

"Love the barber upstairs"

— Indicating Mr. Love's second-floor shop, Watertown, N.Y.

— Ridgway, Colo., motel office

When the bell sounds, get out fast

— Washington, D.C., laboratory

Foreign ladies have fits upstairs

— Hongkong second-floor tailor

Bank of the Holy Ghost

—Rome

Eureka Garlic Company

— Mountainside, N.J.

No undershirt allowed in the airport

— Mactan Airport, P.I.

CRYPT FOR TWO, $660

— St. Louis cemetery on busy highway

Let us fill your next prescription. You will be pleasantly surprised.

—Maryland pharmacy

Customers Wanted
No Experience Needed
Apply Within

— New York shop

—Near an Ipswich, Mass., body of water

In the article, "On the Ph. D. in Mathematics," by I.N. Herstein, on page 821, line 26, of the August-September 1969 issue of the Monthly, please read "Damn" instead of "darn."

– American Mathematical Monthly

On a Fishkill, N.Y., road near a school:

Municiple Dump

For Residents

and

Garbage Only

Protect Our

SLOW

Children

– West Amwell, N.J.

Breakfast is obligatory. No deduction possible. Our clients are requested to take it in the cafe restaurant.

– Grand Hotel Winkler, Salzburg

Try Our Sirloins, For Goodness Steaks!

> — *New York restaurant*

JAIL KEYS MADE HERE

> — *Ohio locksmith*

Boys' Genes For Sale

> — *Dearborn, Mich.*

No one under eighteen admitted without proof of age

> — *New York box office*

Milton, Mass., restaurant:

YE OLDE BROWNE JUG
Chinese Food

ENTRANCE ONLY
DO NOT ENTER

—Penfield, N.Y., parking lot

 *– British road sign*

Above the banana bin at a Corvallis, Ore., supermarket:

> "Please don't break us apart,
> We grew up together"

"Intimate Apparatus"

– Lingerie department in Galeries Lafayette, Paris

A mineral spring in Jamaica, West Indies, is advertised as Good for authoritis.

On a vacant lot near Boulder, Col.:

FOR SALE SHOWN BY APPOINTMENT

On the trash baskets in Edinburgh, Scotland:

"The amenity of our streets
is recommended to your care"

Mayflower Furniture
30 Years Without a Sale

— Newton, Mass.

Cook Book Cake
Made from a cook book recipe

— Highland, N.J., bakery

DEFENSE PROCEDURES FOR ELEVATOR NO. 4

Take shelter — pick up wardens from
floors 2 through 5 and take to first
floor. Return to basement.
(Note: in case of actual emergency,
elevators will not operate.)

— Colorado Springs

Please Do Not Block Exit
It is the Only Entrance in Or Out

— *Chicago shoe repair shop*

We Curl Up and Dye For You

— *Rockport, Mass., beauty shop*

On Sale: Early American Hollywood Bed

— *Washington, D.C., furniture store*

— *Virginia hot dog shack*

To Better Serve You We Now Permit Tipping

— *Nedick's, N.Y.C.*

A Stuart, Va., going-out-of-business sign:

WE UNDERSOLD EVERYONE

Sorry—no parking meter duplicate keys made

— New York locksmith

In restrooms in library of U. of Colorado, Boulder:
State Law does not require *non*-food handlers to wash their hands, but it is the *civilized* thing to do.

Pants pressed here. A shilling a leg. All seats free

— London tailor shop

Undergoing Surgery for Growing Pains

– Springfield, Mo., hospital renovations

In the window of a Lower East Side butcher shop:

"This is the store of Max the Knife."

– In tourist-class washroom of Greek ship Arkadia

In case of emergency, call any of the
following persons in the order listed –

– Albany, Cal.

Booths will be occupied by customers
during the lunch hour only by customers
wishing to eat their meals.

– Lubbock, Tex., restaurant

Notary Public with seal in the rear

— Warren, Mich.

NOTICE

1th.   This Hotel 'll be not responsible for losts of any valuables ocurred on the rooms. That are not deposited on registering.

2th.   Please be sure you deposit your valuables on the administration from 9 a.m. to 2 p.m. and from 4 p.m. to 6 p.m. we are not responsible losts of woods. That are not deposited there. Sunday from 9 a.m. to 2 p.m.

3th.   Please report your take out before 3 p.m. due time to check your leaving.

4th.   Please ask to your own servants no to use the swiming pool that is esclusive for guest.

5th.   The swimming pool is open fromm 7 a.m. to 10.30 p.m.

6ht.   Guest are no allwed to keep kichen devises or any other electric gadgets inside the rooms. That may endanger the Hotels safety

7ht.   It is estrictly forbiden to receive any outside

calls after 8 p.m. we reserve the right to stop them visitors. Here.

8ht.   Any thing broken or despoiled in the rooms and other facilies offered for your confort in this Hotel will be charged to your bill of account

9ht.   Please don't take out the towels from your rooms, In case if you loose any towel we have to chargeiton your bill.

10th,   Any complaint will be atended to for the manger on charge of this hotel

11th.   Any guest that causes an inconvenience to the Hotel and that dangers the security of the guest of the Hotel will have to move by order af the manager and clerk.

12th.   We are not autorized to accept any personal cheks.

13th   The guets please every friday or saturday paid your balance.

THE ARE REGULATIONS OF THE HOTEL

– Acapulco

GOOFS
IN PRINT

At a White House luncheon given by Mrs. Nixon, the President popped in between the creeps and the fruit to joke with the guests.

—Boston Herald-Traveler

YOUNG DEMS TO HEAR DOPE TALK

—Jersey Journal

The muggy heat began to get to the golfers on the back side.

—*San Antonio Express-News*

" . . . But," he said, "black people must have a share in the decision faking."

—*Seattle Times*

Members of the family kindly request mourners to omit floral tributes. The deceased was allergic to flowers.

—*Daily Mining Gazette*

Dr. J. C. Pickett showed a film and talked on removing and transporting injured persons to a dinner and business meeting of District 13 of Ohio Funeral Directors Association.

—*Newark (O.) Advocate*

The St. Louis Audubon Society
will hold its annual bird census
Saturday in St. Charles, Mo.
Following the census, the
group will be served chicken
dinner.

—United Press International

Wanted: Girl to run snack bar
at nudist resort in exchange
for room, board, and tips.

—Miami Herald

Parents wishing babies on Palm
Sunday or Easter please contact the pastor for instructions.

—Battle Ground, Ind., church bulletin

Miniature Chihuahuas. 3 lbs.
when fully grown. Also stud
service. Good for asthma.

—Stillwater (Okla.) News-Press

The Voter's Guide will contain brief biological sketches of the candidates.

—Columbus Dispatch

SUMMER SWIM CAN BE MARRED BY DROWNING

—California Altadenan-Pasadenan

When Sarah Bernhardt played this theater she wouldn't go on unless they delivered half her salary in gold bouillon before the show.

—Playbill

This way to Buisness Office.

—Time-Life Building directory

FATHER OF ELEVEN FINED FOR NOT STOPPING

—Boston Herald auto accident story

I do not want to wind up
full of holes in a rice patty.

> —*Jackson (Mich.) Bugle interview
> with draft protester*

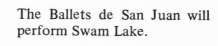

The Ballets de San Juan will
perform Swam Lake.

> —*San Juan Star*

South African Lobster Tail
— From the clear waters of
the Caribbean.

> —*Bronxville, N.Y., inn menu*

Wash face in morning and neck
at night.

> —*Fortune cookie advice*

The Bahamas is a playground
for peripathetic pleasure-
seekers.

> —*New York Times*

Dr. Joseph Peck, born in the last quarter of the nineteenth century, was one of the first doctors in the Connecticut desert, which was only settled after 1900.

> *—German edition of Life With Women And How to Survive It, by Dr. Peck*

If it rains Saturday the picnic will be held the day before.

> *—Salina, Kan., church bulletin*

Give infants particular care. Put them in a sturdy car bed or bassinet. Avoid holding them in arms, and never by the driver.

> *—New Mexico Motori*

COEDS PRESENT UNTIED FRONT IN BERKELEY PROTES

> *—National Observer*

Take a clean dry test tube
half full of water . . .

—*Gilbert chemistry set instructions*

The story is told with zest and
humor by a young English
author, who writes as well as
she handles skis.

—*On front jacket of*
Dead Men Don't Ski

Patricia Moyes came to write
Dead Men Don't Ski when she
was laid up with a dislocated
foot, the result of a skiing
accident.

—*Back jacket, Dead Men Don't Ski*

How To Hire, Handle, and Hold Your Secretary

—*Management Methods (magazine*
article)

There is a raft of strangle new
income tax situations.

—*Commerce Clearing House*
newsletter

Mrs. Leonard sustained lacerations of the month when her automobile ran off the road.

—Norwalk (Conn.) Hour

The truth About Marilyn Monroe! Written by the great American journalist, Robert Frost! Starting Tuesday!

—Advertisement in France-Soir

NO PARKING PROHIBITED WITHOUT A PERMIT

—U. of Cal. San Diego lot

Miss Fortune Befell, another leading U.S. hope in the Olympic women's ski events.

—Waterbury (Conn.) Republican

The Sullivan Award went to Patrolman Vincent Kelly who, alone on August 1, trailed and disarmed a dangerous melon.

—Boston Herald

Mr. and Mrs. Joseph T. Fraser, Jr. of Philadelphia are pictured at Delphi, Greece, where they exploded antiquities.

—Philadelphia Inquirer

Flying not only expedites her daily business, but has given her the deepest personal satisfaction she has had since the death of her husband several years ago.

—Florida TV Week magazine

Photography instructor William Eckenberg will be heaving dinner with President Johnson in Washington.

—Valley Stream, N.Y., church bulletin

Quonset Sailing Camps. Cape Cod camp for girls 7 to 15 featuring daily sailing on beautiful Pleasant Boy.

—New York Times

To prepare for the arrival of 17,000 boy scouts and explorers, scout officials said that mountain trails have to be cleared, remote mountain camps have to be reopened, and officers have to be cleaned.

—Albuquerque Journal

You expect more from American and you get it. (Printed in Japan)

Shirley Englehorn, playing out of Palm Desert, California, shot a small gathering at wind-whipped Pleasant Valley Country Club.

The stock market may be taking time to catch its breast.

Some graduating students at the Rhode Island School of Design don't like the design of their new diploma: a 19th Century French painting of a nude woman. The design is a bleak and white reproduction of a nude by Jean Ingres.

Mobile Home for Rent. Air conditioned, like new, 2 bedroom, large cabana. Water, garbage furnished.

—Lakeland (Fla.) Ledger

You are cordially invited to a luncheon presented by The Family Fitness Council at the Plaza, New York City. Please join us in exploring mind, body and utilization aspects of personal fitness. Cocktails 11:30 A.M.

—Press announcement

The men I have talked to over here feel much as I do. We support the peace marchers whole-heatedly.

—Miami Herald

High School girl wants job after 3 and weekends. Good typist, excellent grammer.

—Beaumont (Tex.) Enterprise

Man's first close-up photographs of the moon's Ocean of Storms—a bleak, dull-gray expense strewn with rocks—were released Thursday.

—*Detroit Free Press*

Smith, Kline & French Laboratories disclosed Tuesday it will donate $1 million worth of drugs to Biafra. Spokesmen said the drugs primarily are vitamins, iron supplements and tranquillizers.

—*Orlando (Fla.) Sentinel*

The new hostel in Berkeley is not associated with any youth hostile association.

—*San Francisco Chronicle*

As the 15-inch snowfall clogged the streets, most New Yorkers kept their cars parked yesterday. But a few hardy soles took to the street in an effort to get to work.

—*Louisville Courier-Journal*

The judge will have the power
to order removed any dog that
commits a fragrant error.

—*Instructions in obedience
school text*

"The differences between Mr.
Crosby and I arise over the
question . . ."

—*Letter in Publishers' Weekly,
from the President of the
Authors Guild*

Middle age woman with car
wants sleep in housekeepers
job with refined gentleman
preferred till she can get her
father's estate.

—*Long Island Press*

A mediocre but interested
audience heard the outstanding
address of Jack L. Miller of
Parkersburg.

—*Ritchie County (W. Va.) Gazette*

Rent. Hall with kitchen and toilet (can seat 100 persons) or could be converted into dwelling place.

—*London Express*

General Westmoreland attended and was a graduate of that famous American military school, Fort Knox.

—*Swiss radio broadcast*

Act III. Scene 2. Recollection. To indicate that naked human love rises above nationality, Cho-Cho and officer wear tights only.

—*Tokyo ballet program for Madame Butterfly*

All funeral coaches must pull to the curb and stop when the siren sounds, although the occupants are not required to seek shelter.

—*Civil Defense air-raid instructions*

"Father Joe." Autobiography of a monster of the Church of England and his work in the London slums.

—Publishers' Weekly

A student who has a plan for a specific activity in lieu of regular class attendance may be executed with written parental permission.

—Princeton Packet

As the hearing in 57th District Court concerning obscenity at a local bookstore unfolded, Judge Franklin Spears suddenly halted the proceedings and stated: "Mr. Quinlan, if you wouldn't refer to the genitals as gentiles, I would appreciate it."

—San Antonio Express

There is less than 5 percent chance of today and tomorrow.

—Louisville Times weather prediction

The Advent Season held special significance for the University of Delaware Computing Center. As the shepherds and Wise Men of 2,000 years ago rejoiced in the coming of the long-awaited King of Kings, so today do faculty, students, associates, and friends of the University of Delaware rejoice in the arrival of the long-awaited computer system on campus.

—*Newark (Del.) Compiler*

The American Bar Association at long last has endorsed legislation providing for the removal of federal judges guilty of misconduct or suffering physical or mental ability.

—*Albuquerque Journal*

Concerning U.S. strictness in requiring proof of financial support for visas, no country likes to admit a foreigner who may be indignant.

—*Whittier (Cal.) Carillon*

This is an artist's conception
of a $2-million DC10 simulator
that will be used to train crows
to fly the 300-passenger airbus.

—Cleveland Plain Dealer

Jerry Korn has been appointed
editor of Time-Life Books. He
succeeds Maitland Edey, under
whom a total of 161 titles were
produced and 30 copies were
sold.

—Book Production Industry

STORM OVER SEX EDUCATION SAID TO BE PETERING OUT

St. Thomas (V.I.) News

May we present again this
morning Miss Elizabeth Wilson
whose engagement and ap-
proaching marriage to the
wrong man were announced
on Friday morning.

—Lincoln (Neb.) Journal

There is so much DDT in the
human body that it is unfit
for human consumption.

—Junction City (Kan.) Argus

"Battle 1066" by Brig. General
C. N. Barclay. The background,
occurrences, and aftermath of
the Battle of Hastings. Photographs.

—Eugene (Ore.) Register-Guard

Honeymoon Suite $28. Each
additional person $2.

— Valdosta, Ga., motel directory

The coroner had spread the
contents of the pockets out on
an end table . . . the usual junk:
a key ring, some small change,
a wallet with two twenties and
four three's.

*—The Twisted Thing, by
Mickey Spillane*

Dancing housegirl, 28, seeks penfriend, 35–40, view matrimony. Likes children. Good figure, jolly, no children, no head lice, no stealer, not frigid.

—New Zealand Press

Lasagna instead of spaghetti 40 cents. No Substitutions.

—Binghamton, N.Y., Villa menu

United Nations Peace Mugs. A most appreciated gift and a good influence on the table. $1.50. (American Made. Beware of Japanese Imitations.)

—American Home

Moscow.—A top Soviet scientist not only approves of computer dating, he believes it expedient to use computers to help people choose a souse.

—New York Post

Beeville, Texas.—Experts agree that the old theory that bees know their master is a myth. Most bees do not live long enough to recognize a keeper, and a wise keeper doesn't visit the hive very often. An average hive is estimated to contain 0,000 bees.

—*Philadelphia Inquirer*

The highlight of the evening, however, will be the drowning of the Queen and her four court members.

—*Alliance (O.) Review*

The Coconut Grove Neighborhood Development Project at a glance: Goals—Repair and modernize homes, tear down and build dilapidated structures.

—*Miami Herald*

For Sale: Stainless steel clam cooker. Capacity 35 people.

—*Sarasota Islander*

Order our rings by mail. State
size or enclose string tied
around finger.

—*Mail order catalog*

For the other two compositions
to be presented Wednesday
evening, Seattle Symphony
Conductor Milton Ratims has
selected Bach-Schonberg's
Prelude in E-flat Major, and
Beethoven's "Erotica" Symphony No. 3 in E-flat Major.

—*Tacoma News Tribune*

TWO HIGH FRENCH GENERALS SUSPENDED OVER GUNBOATS

—*Boston Globe*

Hannah Stringer desires information on Nancy Crumley and
sisters Annie and Rachel,
brothers John and Ben. Annie
had a birthmark looked like a
coconut inside of left thigh
just above the knee, last seen
71 years ago in Arkansas.

—*The Genealogical Helper*

Private Organ Lessons in a
Group. $1.00. Sign up Now!

—*Ithaca Journ*

Speaking with a distinct accent
and looking younger than his
68 years, Rene Jules Dubos
was born in Saint Brice, France,
on February 20, 1901.

—Today's Health

Barney Shulman converted a
pair of fowl shots tonight to
give L.I.U. a 50–49 victory
over Bridgeport.

—New York Times

I shutter every time I think of
exposing our kids to teachers
like that.

—Houston Post

Kenneth Rogers was sentenced
to 75 to 100 years in prison
today after pleading guilty to
the strangulation murders of his
wife and her woman compan-
ion. Before passing sentence,
Judge John Clayton informed
Rogers of his gal rights and
asked if he wanted more time.

—Mattoon (Ill.) Journal Gazette

State of the Union Messages: 1790–1966. Compiled and indexed for the first time, these documents present a weeping view of American history.

—Barnes & Noble (publisher's announcement)

Expansa-Fence. Children are safely enclosed, but not confined, with this super-sized gate-type fence that expands to form a playground 5″ in diameter.

—Creative Playthings catalog

Hashington, D.C. (AP)–Opponents of proposed war curbs . . .

Concord (N.H.) Monitor

ALLEN'S GOAL: END
ILLITERCY IN U.S.

—New York Post

Help Wanted—Men and women, ages 18 to 60 to work in Orleans County. Must be neat. Car essential but not necessary.

—*Newport (Vt.) Express*

John Tushaus, a former University of Arizona star, recalls that as a schoolboy javelin thrower in Montana he acquired the sum total of his instruction by studying sequential pictures of a man throwing the javelin in an encyclopedia.

—*Sports Illustrated*

We have taken all precautions to print, assemble, and package your business forms to your specifications. Each of us, who worked on your order, is aware that your business forms are our business and your satisfaction is our guarantee of continued success. We aim to serve you continuously with a quality product. Sincerely, 2050.

—*Moore Business Forms Inc., letter*

Since the time of the inception of the Order, we have become international in scope. We now include Canada and women.

—Sons of Norway Viking

Mini-Festivals Would Restrict Drugs and Sex: Affairs Would Be Controlled Better.

—Narrowsburg (N. Y.) News-Times

RESTRAIN JET HOSTESSES
New Giant Liners Require Varied Techniques

Wanted for one evening, use of loft wall on which to paint mural. No charge to you.

—New York Times

—South Bend (Ind.) Tribune

REFORM RABBINIC BODY TO HOLD ITS 81ST ANNUAL FIRST CONVENTION IN ISRAEL

—Brooklyn American Examiner

As a result of pressures from special interest groups, such as nudist colonies, we've had to become much more permissive over the past five years. Then we wouldn't develop shots of nude women with public hair showing. Now we will.

—New York Post

In Alaska, comfortable walking shoes are a must. In 586,000 square miles there's a lot of ground you'll want to cover.

—Los Angeles Times

The Choraleers performed Handel's oratorio, "Messiah," at Spaulding High School auditorium Sunday night to a near-capacity crowd, aided by the Choraleer Strings. The event marked the beginning of the Advent season, a religious feast that coincides with the Christmas shopping days.

—Barre (Vt.) Times-Argus

Now the government has accepted responsibility for pollution in public speeches.

—*New Scientist*

But Wilbur Mills is beginning to see that poverty is an infectious disease, and so is the President.

—*New York Times*

Joseph Sills, 49, convicted of robbing a dry cleaners, was sentenced Tuesday by Criminal District Judge Chamberlain to 1,000 years in prison. Sills had served previous sentences for similar offenses.

—*Dayton (O.) News*

The four ages of man are childhood, youth, adultery, and old age.

—*Learning to Live (textbook)*

Pastor Bjorge will be having the Morning Medication on Radio Station KDMA every morning at 11:15.

—*Granite Falls, Minn., church letter*

CREATIVE WRITING OFTEN HAMPERS POOR SPELLER

—*Fremont (Neb.) Tribune*

There are indications that Secretary of Transportation Volpe will stand by his decision to halt construction of Interstate 93 short of Franconia Notch. Conservationists claim the $60 million stretch of road will damage the unique theological museum at the north end of the narrow gap.

—*Boston Globe*

In the Romanian market there is powerful competition between foreign firms wishing to sell their goo.

—*Wall Street Journal*

Senator McGovern said President Nixon has proclaimed a goal of seeing that a free lunch is provided to every American child who needs it by next Thanksgiving.

—Associated Press

All errata are being incorporated into the test.

—Publisher's announcement of revised edition, Palace of Minos at Knossos

The Ohio Supreme Court today upheld two lower court opinions that approved a payment schedule for a husband to buy his widow's property.

—Newark (O.) Advocate

Position available for Emotionally Disturbed Teacher.

—Trenton Times

A rugged, red-bearded student beat out his lady opponent, Nancy Wong, for the presidency of the Associated Women Students at Hartnell Junior College in Salinas, California. Although the group's constitution bars male members, it does not stimulate the sex of its president.

—Detroit Free Press

Casalpalocco. Little cottage, garden, 3 bedrooms, 3 bathrooms, living, dining room, kitchen. Upstairs cellar.

—Rome Daily American

ROTARY PROJECT IS DRUG ABUSE

—Los Angeles Times

The brakes on a gasoline tanker truck apparently failed early yesterday and the truck rolled into a pharmacy, caught fire and exploded. Police said the truck driver had left the rig to eat a nearby diner in this Long Island north shore community.

—Boston Herald-Traveler

The bomb, black power in a small can, went off under the unoccupied squad in the parking lot of the Damen avenue detective headquarters.

—Chicago Tribune

Arlington. A wonderful over-sized brick Cape, 4 bedrms, guilt-edged location, yet lower 30's.

—Boston Globe

The women's committee of the Chicago Historical Society visited Williamsburg. Twenty odd ladies made the trip.

—Society announcement

CORRECTION: In the County School Spelling Bee set for March 21, we misspeleld the name of one of the Blue Ridge contestants. Kathy Dixon was School Champion. Her age is 11, and she is in the fifth grade.

—McKinney (Tex.) Examiner

A proposed trip to South Africa by 25 Kansas lawmakers and their wives has been canceled. The trip has somehow become mixed up with the fate of a bill that would have allowed pari-mutuel petting in Kansas.

—Kansas City Star

For Sale. Reconditioned Steinway Baby Grand. The Instrument of the Immorals.

—Burlington (Ont.) Record

For Sale—New sets of Corpus Juris Secundum, Vernon's Annotated Missouri Statutes, and full set of Missouri Practice. Recently purchased by deceased attorney.

—Journal of Missouri Bar

The Lakers then battled on even terms with Boston before falling apart in the final sex minutes.

—Los Angeles Times

After full consultation with the National Security Council, Ambassador Bunker, General Abrams and my other admirers, I have concluded that the actions of the enemy in the last 10 days clearly endanger the lives of Americans.

—President Nixon,
in The New York Times

"No, suh!" Agnew replied with much emphasis and an exaggerated Southern accident.

—Seattle Post-Intelligencer

Opening Tonight! Saida and Ahmad. Renounced Middle Eastern Dance Team.

—Portland Oregonian

The Vermont man slammed into a guard rail while engrossed in a conservation with his dog.

—*Redford (Mich.) Record*

"Most of the men in the country despise styles," said the wife of Attorney General Mitchell."Men are very hard to become adjusted to changes." What about her husband? "He likes anything I war," she said.

—*New York Times*

The reason for mail carriers' low wages is the fact that postal workers don't earn very much.

—*Los Angeles Times*

Tour the South! Male and Female Only.

—*Daily Oklahoman*

In fact, said the report, if you are doomed to be murdered there is a 90 percent chance it will be someone of your own race. Also, your killer is most likely to be someone you know —relative, husband, wife, lover, friend, axquaintance.

—*St. Louis Globe-Democrat*

Almost overnight, this tropical island of Singapore—27 miles wide and 14 miles long—became first-page news.

—*U.S. News and World Report*

Abdollah Ranjbar, a 16-year-old Iranian farmer, divorced his 42-year-old wife after 2 years of marriage and 18 children because she refused to produce a 19th child.

—*San Francisco Chronicle*

Laverne Hanover, Kat Byrd, and Bye Bye Sam lead a list of 17 hores kept eligible for the $94,000 Realization Pace at Roosevelt Raceway on May 30.

—Washington Post

Moms of Twins
Have Program
On Self-Defense

—LaGrange (Ill.) Citizen

CURATOR DESCRIBES
WILDLIFE TO LIONS

—Allentown (Pa.) Call

In two of these books, Ruth and Esther, curiously enough, the heroines are women.

—The Five Megilloth and Jonah

All graduate students expecting to take the comprehensive examination for Ph.D. must be registered at the time he takes the examination.

—U. of Colorado memo

Meals without rice five cents extra.

—*Chinese restaurant menu, New York*

Odd Jobs: Boy wanted to rape and help widow in back yard. Must be clean.

—*South Bend Bulletin*

Gov. John A. Burns, also a Catholic, has until next week to sign or veto the abortion bill or allow it to become law without his signature. He has said he will take the latter curse.

—*Hartford Courant*

Senator Henry L. Bellmon, R—Okla., showed a positive reaction to a tuberculosis skin test in the massive testing on Capitol Hill. The wholesale testing began after two Capitol employees died of TV and several others caught the disease.

—*Atlanta Journal*

Tenders will be received by the undersigned up to noon April 14 for sale of a 2 ton wench.

—The Coast Guard weekly

Please make a note of your social security number and return it to me. Jane B. Allen, Payroll Supermisor.

—New York office memo

FUNERAL SET

FOR CYCLIST

HIT BY ROAD

—San Jose (Cal.) Mercury

United States bombing, according to the general and his deputy for operations, Col. Bounchanh Savathphayphane, halts at a strip three miles from the eastern edge of town. Details on obituary page.

—New York Times

Need love seat or small ouch.
Not longer than 5 feet.

It's nothing special, chef
Sigmund Steber said, just some
meatballs, egg rolls, cold
canopies, shrimp.

—Miami Herald

KICK DOWN STAIRS ENDS FRIENDSHIP

—Toronto Telegram

Georgetown—Brk. Family tree-
house, 6 bedrooms, 3½ baths.

—Washington Post

Rubenstein was charged
with possession of two hypo-
dermic needles, possession
of narcotics implements
(three scales, a hasish pipe,
and spoon) maintaining a
criminal nuisance, possession
of zyyrssuczzzczzzcbyylebsa.

—Yonkers Herald

Hal Lanier hit a grandslam
homer as the Giants walloped
the Athletics, 14-14, in an
exhibition game.

—San Francisco Chronicle

We had nine meetings during
the year. February was can-
celled due to the weather.

—Helena, Mont., parish report

JAYCEES

ENCOURAGE

SEWER TALK

—Jackson (Mich.) Citizen-Patriot

The Cougars hit 38 of 36 free
throws in this foul-infested
contest.

—Houston Post

It was General Manager John
Fox, a Sevier County native
who formerly served as director
of pubic relations at Carson-
Newman College, who decided
on the new theme.

—Knoxville Journal

Full time permanent position available for mature, responsible person. Peasant working conditions.

—Northern Virginia Sun

MAO RULE
SAID SHITFED

—Los Angeles Times

Room for horse—Small 3 bedroom, one acre.

—Lake Oswego (Ore.) Review

We want to apologize for our errotic service.

—Saturday Review

Monday, Tuesday and Wednesday Evenings Only! $20 Permanent $10. $20 Frosting $10. Reg. $9 Touchup $6.50. This is our sincere attempt to assist in President Nixon's inflation program.

—Wayne (Pa.) Suburban

DIPLOMAT DUBCEK HAILED
BY TURKEY'S RIGHT WING

—Columbus (O.) Dispatch

The chancel choir will sing two Negro spirituals, and the chancel choir will sing "Surely, He Hath Borne Our Briefs."

—Orrville (O.) News

In his Silent Spot, Skelton invades an Irish pub, and the Baja Marimba Band performs between skirts. (1 hour)

—Long Island Daily Press

Help Wanted. Part Time Male. General office cleaning.

—Westchester (N.Y.) News

If the socks are light in color, the fuzz probably results from abrasion between the two fibers. The fluffy wool flexes against the firmer nylon and is worn off. Washington floats the severed fibers to the surface.

—Christian Science Monitor

REVOLTING WOMEN TO BE CONFERENCE THEME

—Detroit News

Beth Woodward is the 1969
candidate for the American
Broad program of the American Field Service.

—Massena (N.Y.) Observer

Carol Mitchell, socialist with
Texas Girls Choir, is touring
Europe.

—Dallas Morning News

Vermont Land, circa Lake
Champlain, skiing, God.

—Saturday Review

When asked by Rep. Robert
Leggett, Democrat of California, whether the Administration contemplated having any
American forces in Cambodia
after July 1, the President
reportedly replied: Give fun
for someone. Give to the Fresh
Air Fund.

—New York Times

What Dayton needs is one very good opposition newspaper edited by a god, conservative editor.

—*Dayton (O.) News*

The Communists are making an all-out effort to put *Catch Her in the Rye* in every U.S. high school.

—*Lewiston (Mont.) Argus*

Vasectomy—male sterilization —is a simple operation that can be done in 15 minutes in a doctor's office. And the anticipated cost is $200—the price of a trombone.

—*Guelph (Ont.) Mercury*

Buyers with less than 20% down will pay 8 3/4% interest, plus mortgage insurance and other fees. All qualified home owners will expire after the loan is contrast with the previous Marine policy.

—*Milwaukee Journal*

A San Francisco woman is donating $3 in paintings by Gauguin, Manet, Matisse, and Renoir to the De Young Museum.

—Houston Post

Royal Air Force Arctic Mittens. Special Purchase. Limited Quality.

—New York Times

Charles Manning, Fork Union Magisterial Distrist representative on the Fulvanna County Board of Supervisors, said he objected to the fact that the books refer to incidents which happened a hundred years ago. He added he is not opposed to a black literature program, but "for God's sake give us some history we can be proud of."

—Richmond Times-Dispatch

Dr. Paul B. Waller, associate professor of education at the University of Virginia, claims that young people in this cataclysmic era cannot stand poverty. "There's a concerted effort to destroy what we have taken 300 years to build."

—Roanoke (Va.) Times

The police dislike the hippies because they conjugate in groups.

—Westminster (Cal.) Report

HARPER FILES

OBSCENE SUIT

—Pensacola (Fla.) Journal

Seven married men build luxury yachts in this small suth coast town have quit work because they say the job has made them lose their sex drive. Peter Webster, their boatyard boss, said the impotency idea arose after they read something about it in the papers—they panickled.

—New York Post

An inter-collegiate composers symposium will be held Saturday November 15 in the Rectal Hall, San Fernando Valley State College.

—Composer and Conductor

They left the vessel wearing what they had on when they got out of bed. Some were barefoot. Many had blankets draped about their shoulders. Passengers in several lifeboats sank to pass the time.

—Boston Globe

The finest moisturizer you can give your face, Liquid Revenescence, at an introductory price special, $7.50. You can save half on this great Charles of the Titz dry skin moisturizer.

—Oklahoma Journal

Comedian Jackie Gleason and Beverly McKittrick, a bland former secretary, will be married Saturday.

—Milwaukee Journal

The city's Department of Air Resources said that more than 0.10 parts of sulphur dioxide in every million parts of air was considered a healthy hazard.

—New York Times

Avianca flight 780 from Columbia, South America, touched down at Miami International Airport Monday afternoon with a strange cargo. Hundreds of snakes, iguanas and other jungle creatures were bedded down on sacks of marijuana. Two days later the man who was to get the 17 crates of writhing boa constrictors, monkeys and tropical birds was found dead. He had been shot in the head and stuffed into the trunk of an abandoned car. "It looks like there is a lot more to it," a Dade County detective said.

—Tampa Tribune

Howe Mortuary, Spruce at Eleventh
Our Growth Depends on You

—Boulder (Colo.) Camera

A man went into a restaurant and ordered food. The service was slow, so the customer took a knife and pushed it at the waiter, telling him to hurry. The knife went in too far and the waiter bled to death.

—Saudi Arabian crime story

Inasmuch as not even galley proofs are not available, I am not able to criticize the contents of Jim's book.

—Minneapolis Tribune

Movie—Biography. "Lust .for Life" (1956) The life of the great pianist Van Gogh.

—TV Guide

ARMY TRIES A NEW IDEA

—Washington Post

WOMEN'S LIBERATION
REALLY IS BROAD-BASED

—Chicago Sun-Times

President Nixon delivers a campaign speech at Miami Convention Hall. Ghostly and menacing presence.

—Miami Herald TV listing

By seven years later, in 1782, Sarah Siddons was a success and, despite some ups and downs, remained so until her final performance as Lady Macbeth in 1912.

—Publishers' Weekly

The Cape Cod Electric Company will install a new electrostatic precipitator to improve air pollution.

—Radio Station WOCB

Radiation has become a fourth
"r" in the nation's schools in an
effort to stimulate a desire
among students to become
unclear scientists.

—Hamilton (O.) Journal-News

GREENVILLE'S LARGEST WHORESALE
CASH AND CARRY OUTLET

—South Carolina newspaper ad

The automobile is geared
toward a young housewife
with a family looking for a
second war.

—New York Times

Movie: *Deep Blue Sea*, Vivian
Leigh. A confused society
married woman has a tragic
and tortured love affair with
a horse below her in class.

—San Francisco Examiner-Chronicle

After the plane failed to gain enough altitude, the three passengers got out.

—Ann Arbor News

A recent Yucca Naturist Club newsletter in announcing a social event urged "everyone to bring a covered dish."

—Associated Press

When Lyndon Baines Johnson left Washington, he was seen off at the airport by only a small group of well-washers.

—WNDT-TV

Mr. Eugenc Talmadge, if he was living today, would turn over in his grave when he sees the state of Georgia's budget.

—James Smith, Mayor of Albany, Ga.

AURIAC, 1952 NOBEL PRIZE WINNER, IS DEAD FRANCOIS

—New York Times

SWEDISH DEMONSTRATORS
HURL EGGS, EPITAPHS

—Berkeley Gazette

Describing one of Hitler's mass rallies in Nuremberg, Albert Speer recalls: I divided the fag-bearers into 10 massive columns.

—New York Times

A thunderous burst of apple-sauce greeted Chiang.

—Newark News

Wanted: Organist (male) at least 50 who doesn't resent playing Welk-type music. Must have been legally married at least once. Must be reliable with no drinking problem. Ability to read would be nice.

—International Musician

Following the ceremony, a reception was hell at the Sunset lodge, Norwood.

—Potsdam (N.Y.) Courier & Freeman

5 rms, 3rd flr. Rent with option to buy, $115. Children welcome, but must be husband and wife.

—Boston Globe

Governor Cargo was introduced to the open air fathering of an estimated 300 Indians.

—El Paso Times

Senator McCarthy has established residence in a three-story rented townhouse in Georgetown. In the morning he whips into the kitchen and fries a lot of bacon to go with his English muffin and own steaks, and mixes a salad while sipping a gin and tonic. Three times a week he starts the day with a slick game of tennis at the St. Albans Tennis Club, playing with college-age coffee. At night he broils his neighbors who lives down the street.

—Green Bav (Wis.) Press-Gazette

Channel 13: Making Things
Grow. Unusual pot ideas.

—TV Guide

Some 5,095 stewardesses and
281 pursuers were affected.

—Kansas City Star

Studies of scripture show there
were destitute cities, even to
the making of straw without
brick.

—Radio Station WHDH, Boston

The guests at the charter
dinner of the Edinburgh
Merchant Company wore stiff
shirts, white ties, and tales.

—New York Times

The Committee wish to apolo-
gise to patrons for inconvenience last Sunday night owing
to bust mishap.

—Canterbury, England, announcement

Movie: "A Kiss Before Drying."

—Norfolk (Va.) Ledger-Star

The British pound today moved within a whiskey of the official ceiling of $2.42.

—UPI dispatch

Last week, American Airlines won permission to convert the back end of the plane into a 17-seat lunge with stand-up bar.

—Boston Globe

Cape Cod residents opposed to the prospect of a petport in their backyard are being urged to air their protest.

—Boston Globe

Quick Sandwich. Drain Maine sardines, mash and season sharply with lemon juice, chili sauce, and tobacco. Spread on toast for a quick, high protein sandwich.

—Greenwich (Conn.) News

Now let us talk about the visiting team. This should comprise between three and four persons selected by the initiator.

—Research and
Development magazine

Selection of wooden salad bowels greatly reduced.

—Pensacola News-Journal

In a time when pornography has been defended with the claim that smut is what people want, the ironic fact is that the Bible beats them all year after year.

—Toronto Telegram

O'Henry's Inn is offering a Duffer's (Golfer's) Holiday Special for $349,000.

—*Toronto Globe and Mail*

Did you know that the lights on the Christmas tree have religious significance? The blue ones stand for courage, the red for sacrifice, the white for truth and the green for immorality.

—*Mexico, Mo., church newsletter*

INMATE ARTIST TO BE HUNG IN NEW YORK

—*Colorado State Penitentiary Interpreter*

Raleigh, compared to many Tarheel cities, has a heavy concentration of white-collar professionals and a hefty share of a bustline research center.

—*Raleigh (N.C.) Times*

Mexican-ish Dish: The canned chili should be the kind that contains meat and beans; an added can of cooked roast beef and a few sprinkles of a jar of mayonnaise and one-third of a cherry pie. Taste.

—Rudder

The next meeting of the Castleton Discussion Group will be held Friday at the home of Mrs. Basil Hick. Speaker: William Lyons. Topic: "Are We Emphasizing Formel Education Too Much?"

-Castleton (Md.) News

How to get out of a car in water:

If it is not possible to open the door, roll down the window. The water will pour in but be prepared to wait until the compartment is full in order to equalize the pressure. Then take a deep breath and swim out.

—Houston Chronicle

It was the last trip for the
Zephyr, which rolled out of
Oakland for Salt Lake heading
West.

—Dallas News

Grad Federation Asks Pay Parody

—U. of Colorado Student News

To get more fun out of life,
know your librarian.

—National Library Week publicity

In 1912 he married Jeanne
Lafan, who was to be the
bother of his four children.

—New York Post

Dine and Dance at Ember
Room, White Plains Hotel. Gala
Dinner, Epigrams of Black &
Red Caviar.

—Mamaroneck (N.Y.) Times

CONGRESS LEADERS VOW TO
HUSTLE MORE IN '70 SESSION

—Portland Oregonian

Mr. Elser was born in Irvington
after living in Berkeley Heights
most of his life.

—Newark (N.J.) News

In Warsaw, an American marine
was charged with manslaughter.
Driving an embassy car, he
struck and killed a pole on a
highway 75 miles east of the
city. The pole did not get off
the road at the sight of the car.

—Norwalk (Conn.) Hour

Documentary films, though,
have never been better than
ever.

—Judith Christ, on the Today show

Mrs. Johnson greets the ladies
by first names and is kissed
on the check.

—A Day in the Life of President Johnson

How many people do you
employ, broken down by sex?

*—H.M. Government questionnaire
to firms in Great Britain*

If I can be of further service
to you, please do hesitate to
contact me.

—California State Representatives

Reg. 60¢ Each. Nervous Breakdown. Two for $1.00. As seen
on TV.

—Youngstown (O.) Vindicator

White youths also are rebelling
against adult valves that seem
irrelevant or outmoded.

—Albuquerque Journal

We can't know where we're
going if we don't know where
we are. We means you, too.

—Census bureau

The Shelter offers a mode of college life unlike any other at the university. The Shelter holds about two parties per term, but any occupant may use the social room for an affair of his own if he chooses.

—Pen State Collegian

Help Wanted: Innumerators for new city directary. Must be good spellers, plain writers.

—Wellington (Kan.) News

Elect Arthur Revere Supervisor, Town of Plattsburgh. Experienced—4 Years of Service on the Town Broad.

—Plattsburgh (N.Y.) Press-Republican

Woman with saddle seat, showing and training experience, wishes job with farm.

—New Haven Register